Ip Man

Portrait
of a
Kung Fu Master

Ip Man
Portrait
of a
Kung Fu Master

Ip Ching

Ron Heimberger

Translated by Eric Li

Ip Ching Wing Chun Athletic Association

ISBN 13: 978-1-55517-516-0

Published by King Dragon Press, an imprint of Cedar Fort, Inc.
2373 W. 700 S., Springville, UT 84663
Distributed by Cedar Fort, Inc., www.cedarfort.com

Cover art by Ron Heimberger
Cover design by Adam Ford
Cover design © 2001 by Lyle Mortimer
Typeset by Virginia Reeder
All photos copyright by Ip Ching

Printed in the United States of America

10 9 8 7 6 5 4 3 2 1

I offer this book to the memory of my father and to those at the center of my life, and I offer them my work and my thanks for making it all possible.

—Ip Ching

CONTENTS

Introduction

A Master's gift to the World is his life. By seeing his life or at least by seeing the portrait of his life as painted in the stories of those who knew him a Master's life becomes a sketch of a path to Mastery.

This book paints a portrait of the famous Wing Chun Master, Ip Man. This portrait, woven from stories about Ip Man shared by his son, provides a set of fifteen principles as a guide to mastery. While there are broad lessons to be learned from this portrait remember to savor the details. Many of the great figures of history are shrouded in the mists of aggrandizement, but here the details, the fine strokes of the portrait have remained to show the humble seeker something about the life of a master.

As you will see, each of these chapters provides a principle or set of principles for you to contemplate. You will be richly rewarded if you seek to discern the principles and the man who strove to embody them.

The fifteen principles illustrated in this portrait have not been chosen because they constitute the exclusively necessary principles for mastery. Nor have they been ordered to show a natural progression from one stage of mastery to the next. Instead, they have been chosen to provide you insights into the journey—some landmarks to orient yourself too—drawn from the life of one of the very few truly great Masters.

These principles should draw you into more thought and reflection rather than ending such processes. What has been sketched here, while truly a masterful portrait, is exactly such because it draws you nearer and leaves you desiring to know more.

These stories and the principles drawn from them are commended to you for your benefit and learning and enjoyment. Let them guide you in your journey but do not look for them to tell you every step. Here in this portrait are great treasures for the taking but not simply for the asking.

Grandmaster Ip Man. This photo hangs in the Ving Tsun Athletic Association and specific schools around the world.

Turmoil

"From heaven down to the mass of the people,
all must consider the cultivation of the person being
the root of everything."

—*Unknown*

Ip Kai Man was the third of four children born to Ip Oi Dor and Ng Shui. His older brother was Ip Kai Gak. His older sister was Ip Wan Mei. His younger sister was Ip Wan Hum. Ip Man was born into this wealthy and well-known family in a time of crises that shook the very foundation of China. Ip Man was only two years old when China's Ch'ing Government began to erode. During this time, China lost a war to Japan, which caused panic among the people because foreign powers desired to carve up China for their own gain. At the age of five, Ip Man's world shook once more when the Emperor allowed reform, but the Empress Dowager (along with the top military commander, Jung-Lu) seized the Emperor in a coup d'etat and began her third regency. At the young age of six, Ip Man felt the unrest of the popular Boxer Rising—a movement led by members of a traditional type of secret society called I-ho sh'uan, crudely translated by Westerners as Righteous and Harmonious Fists, or Boxers, who practiced kung fu. This movement, although marginally successful in waging war against the foreign powers seeking to carve up China, led to widespread disorder, riots, banditry, and uprising in every province in China. At the end of the uprising, many Boxers were punished and put to death. Consequently, most kung fu masters assumed a low profile. Ip Man once again felt the tremors that would topple his beloved homeland when, at the age of seven, he saw the first foreign armies occupy Northern China.

By the age of twelve, Ip Man's life was easier. Even though the government was still in upheaval, by the year 1905 the Chinese people had returned to a semblance of normal life—giving Ip Man a window of opportunity to study Wing Chun. It was during this time that a man moved into the Ip family clan hall on the main street (Song Yuen Dai Gai) of Foshan. His name was Master Chan Wa Shun and he had come to the Ip family clan hall to teach kung fu. He was the only non-family member to learn Leung Jan's Wing Chun. Chan Wa Shun was a large and strong man and he always helped others out when they got into fights. So naturally when Master Leung Jan died, everyone thought Mr. Chan was the heir to the Wing Chun system and went to him for Wing Chun instruction—even over Leung Jan's two sons, Leung Chun and Leung Bik (though they may have been more qualified to teach their father's system).

The young Ip Man liked watching classes, and like all young boys, he had no shame in asking if he could learn kung fu from Chan Wa Shun. Chan Wa Shun told him that people who were rich and came from comfortable surroundings made poor students of Wing Chun. But because he was teaching at the Ip family building, Chan Wa Shun could not simply refuse Ip Man's request. So, he reluctantly agreed to teach Ip Man. However, Chan Wa Shun required Ip Man to pay 500 Tai Yeung (Silver Dollars) to become a student. This amount was enough money to buy several houses. Chan Wa Shun knew that such an amount would be almost impossible for a young boy to raise and he thought he had found a way to softly discourage Ip Man. It took Ip Man some time to get this amount of money, yet he did and with money in hand, Ip Man went to see Chan Wa Shun. Chan Wa Shun was shocked. He suspected that Ip Man had stolen the money. Chan Wa Shun immediately took Ip Man to see his father. Ip Man's father explained that he and Ip Man's mother, Ng Shui, had given the boy the money so he could study kung fu from Chan Wa Shun.

From that time forward, Ip Man was an official student of Chan Wa Shun. Though Chan Wa Shun only taught a total of sixteen people, Ip Man had the opportunity to learn directly from Chan Wa Shun for three years before Chan passed away. Thus began Ip Man's journey into Wing Chun. Though he would start from privilege he would, in the end, dedicate everything to the pursuit of Wing Chun. It was a journey that would transcend political upheaval and loss of fortune. And in the end, Ip Man would show that it is not the student's surroundings or background that matter but his heart and his soul.

The street sign that marks the famous Chop Stick Street.
It is where Leung Jan ran his herbal shop.

The Ip Family building is where Chan Wa Shun taught his Wing Chun Class in Foshan China. It is the place where Ip Man began his training as a boy. Unfortunatly the building where Chan Wa Shun taught has been demolished. Today all that remains is a neighborhood park.

Gongzheng Lu is the name of the street where Chan Wa Shun taught his class in Foshan.

Left to right. Kowk Fu, Ip Ching, Lun Kai. Kowk Fu and Lun Kai were students of Ip Man in Foshan. Actually Lun Kai was a boy servant of the Chow family. His master was a student of Ip Man. While Ip Man was teaching Mr. Chow, the boy servant, Lun Kai, would practice with his master. Actually Ip Man did not have any problem with this and continued to let Lun Kai learn Wing Chun along with his master. Lun Kai was about the same age as Ip Ching and they would often practice the Siu Lim Tao together while living in Foshan.

Front gate to St. Stephen's College in Hong Kong. After the death of his Kung fu master, Chan Wa Shun, Ip Man moved to Hong Kong to attend High School at St. Stephen's College. It was during this time that Ip Man met his kung fu older uncle (Si-pak), Leung Bik.

The Refiner's Fire

Some are born with the knowledge of their duties; some know them by study; and some acquire the knowledge after a painful feeling of their ignorance.

—Confucius

With the help of his relative Leung Fut Ting, Ip Man moved to Hong Kong at the age of 15, in 1908, to attend High School at St. Stephen's College. During this time the British, who ruled Hong Kong, were using Indian and Pakistani police officers in Hong Kong. The police were not very fond of the Chinese people and were often quite cruel. One day, on the way to school, Ip Man and a classmate came across an Indian police officer who was beating a Chinese lady. Ip Man had seen all types of injustice but this time he had to do something about it. Both kids told the officer that if this lady was a thief or if she had done something wrong then the policeman had every right to take her into custody. But even if she was a thief, he had no right to beat her. In actuality, she had done nothing wrong. The police officer was just being cruel. And the officer, realizing that Ip Man was just a kid, took a swing at Ip Man. Unfortunately for the police officer, Ip Man had nearly four years of kung fu under his belt. Ip Man responded to the police officer's attack with what appeared to his classmate to be a very simple move, but the police officer went down with blood all over his face. Ip Man and his classmate ran very quickly to school.

The school sign. It was around 1908 when the grandmaster moved to Hong Kong to attend school. It was during this time that Ip Man finished his training in the art of Wing Chun at the hands of his kung fu older uncle, Leung Bik.

Ip Man's classmate told an older man who lived in the same building about what had happened that day. The old gentleman, who was also from Foshan, asked the young man to show him what Ip Man had done. When he saw what the young man showed him, the old man asked Ip Man's classmate to ask Ip Man to come and see him. The next day, both Ip Man and his friend went to see the older gentleman. The older gentleman asked Ip Man what type of kung fu he had studied in Foshan. Ip man replied that it was the best type of kung fu in the world and that if he told him, the old man wouldn't understand. After a little cajoling, Ip Man relented and told the old man that he had studied a famous kung fu called Wing Chun. The older gentleman replied that he had heard of it and that there was a person named Chan Wa Shun teaching there. The old gentleman asked Ip Man to show him the Siu Lim Tao form. After the demonstration the old man said, "Eh, not too great." As you can imagine, Ip Man, who felt he was doing the best kung fu in the world, did not respond favorably to the old man's evaluation of his skill.

The old gentleman then asked Ip Man to perform his Chum Kiu form. One must remember that at this time the respect between young people and older people was greater than it is now. Ip Man, though obviously unhappy with the old gentleman's request, complied anyway, out of respect for the old man. During his demonstration, the old man kept shaking his head and saying, "Not very good." This made Ip Man very, very unhappy. At this point the old man asked Ip Man to demonstrate the Biu Gee form. Not wanting the old man to know he didn't know the Biu Gee form, Ip Man said, "I really don't feel like showing you the form." Then the old man asked if Ip Man would chi sau (Wing Chun's way of fighting) with him. Ip Man happily complied, thinking that he

Grandmaster Ip Man

could finally teach the old man a lesson. Ip Man threw a punch. The old man simply blocked it and threw him to the side. Ip Man got up and attempted to heal his wounded pride with another punch. Once again the old man just blocked him and threw him aside. Ip Man got up and stormed out.

The next day Ip Man's friend told him that the old gentleman wanted to see him. Naturally Ip Man didn't want anything to do with him and he told his friend he would not see the old man. The friend dutifully reported Ip Man's response to the old gentleman. The old gentleman told the teenage boy to let Ip Man know that he was Leung Bik. The next day in class, Ip Man's friend told him the old gentleman was Leung Bik. Right there, even before class was over, Ip Man jumped up and went straight to Leung Bik's home. Ip Man's excitement stemmed from the fact that Leung Bik was Ip Man's Si Pak (older kung fu uncle, the youngest son of his teacher's teacher, Leung Jan.)

Leung Bik was not doing very well financially in Hong Kong. He was living with a relative. Ip Man invited the master to live with him. This Leung Bik did and taught Ip Man the Wing Chun system until 1912 when Leung Bik died. Ip Man learned the entire system of Wing Chun under Leung Bik's guidance. When Leung Bik died, Ip Man returned to Foshan to help his kung fu brothers with the knowledge he had gained in Hong Kong.

Throughout his life, Ip Man referred to Leung Bik as Si Pak. Even though both of his kung fu teachers had the same kung fu, they both had different teaching styles. Chan Wa Shun was a relatively uneducated man whose metaphors and understanding were more grounded in the earth, in the common man's language.

1962. My father and I enjoying the day. This place is near the airport. It is a place where people can go and relax away from people. We could actually watch the planes take off and land from where we sat.

Leung Bik, on the other hand, was very educated and his metaphors and understanding were shaped by philosophy. His understanding of the principles of Wing Chun was deeper and more refined than his kung fu younger brother, Chan Wa Shun.

Though Ip Man learned from both Chan Wa Shun and Leung Bik and though claiming Leung Bik's lineage would have been more impressive, Ip Man never called Leung Bik his Sifu. Ip Man understood the respect that a student should have for his teacher. Ip Man was not opportunistic. He was not interested in climbing the political ladder by taking advantage of the gift that Leung Bik had given him. For Ip Man it was the search for Wing Chun that mattered—not his status in another's eyes.

Grandmaster Ip man, circa 1950

1970. Ip Man relaxes in his home at Tung Choi Street, Hong Kong.

Ip Man circa 1960

The Challenge

*When the mind is not present, we look and do
not see; we hear and do not understand; we eat
and do not know the taste of what we eat.*

—Unknown

Around 1918, a master from Northern China—a Praying
Mantis instructor—came and visited the Jing Mo Wui, of Foshan,
or the martial art sports association of Foshan. At the Jing Mo Wui,
a person could learn Chinese martial arts from a variety of instruc-
tors. After watching for a while, the Praying Mantis master
declared that there was no one capable of teaching Chinese martial
arts in Foshan because no one knew the proper techniques of Kung
Fu. He then threw down a challenge. He would fight any master
from Foshan. Upon hearing the challenge, the town became
confused as to who should represent them. Some wanted the best
masters; however, they were too old. Some wanted the younger
students; however, they were not experienced. They finally asked a
well-known herbal doctor named Lee Kong Hoi if he knew
someone. This was one of Ip Man's friends and so Mr. Lee asked Ip
Man if he could represent the town in the fight. Ip Man's answer
was that if he was not learning Kung Fu to fight and help others out
then why even bother—so he accepted. They set the date and place
of the fight. It was to take place at the theatre where an organizer
would sell tickets and serve hot tea.

Tables were set up and the time for the fight was just one day away. It was at this time that the challenger found out where Ip Man visited every night. The challenger showed up and saw Ip Man and claimed that he could throw Ip Man down with one hand. Then with his specialty, the phoenix fist, he punched the wall, which in that day was made of rock and mortar. His punch left a hole in the wall. Everyone thought that this man had much power. Ip Man just smiled as the challenger left the room. The next day was fight day. Everyone crowded into the outdoor theatre. Nearly two thousand people wanted to see the fight. The audience took their seats with little tables set up between each set of chairs for tea. The referee was to toss a coin to see where the two fighters should start. Ip Man being the challenged had the call and won the toss. He chose to stand with his back to the audience. No one could figure this out since he was a Foshan man and most of the audience was made up of Foshan people. However, the fight began. The challenger attacked with a phoenix fist, as expected. Ip Man countered with a Biu and Lop or thrust, grab and pulling technique. This caused the challenger to fly off the stage and land on one of the tea tables breaking three ribs. The fight was over, but most people came to see a fight. The promoter knew that this could create quite a problem and asked Ip Man if he could do something—maybe a demonstration (for about thirty minutes), of how he defeated the Praying Mantis master. Ip Man agreed and demonstrated the hand forms. This gave the organizer time to organize other demonstrations and lion dances. The whole evening turned out to be a giant party and Ip Man became famous all over Foshan.

Ip Man felt throughout his entire life that Wing Chun was to be used for the benefit of the downtrodden and defenseless. He never treated Wing Chun as a means for self-aggrandizement or as a means for getting rich quickly. When called to stand for the

Ip Man poses with two of his students. From left to right: Wong Kowk Yau, Ip Man, Mak Po.

This photo was taken during class at Heng Yip Building (the Castle Peak Road school). Ip Man always worked out in this type of clothing. His favorite brand of cigarettes were camel. His smoking contributed to his death in 1972.

honor of his city, he gladly accepted. For Ip Man the essence of Wing Chun was honor and courage. And even when others all around him were impressed by the outward displays of this master, Ip Man saw through to the heart of the matter using wisdom against strength and courage against bluster.

Ip Man lived a comfortable life for many years in Foshan after returning from Hong Kong and did not have to work because of his wealth. But when the Japanese invaded, this all ended. Life became harder because Ip Man lost his fortune. The government was literally digging up lawns to find family fortunes buried there. Ip Man needed a job. Because of his fame in Foshan, he was offered the job of police chief for the government in the town. It was just one year earlier that the Ch'ing dynasty had officially ended and the Kuo Min Tang ruled China. Ip Man stayed in this position until the Communist party took control of China and in 1949 he moved back to Hong Kong to avoid the Communist rule in the mainland.

Ip Man's sense of civic virtue had returned to stand him in good stead. Ip Man defended the honor of his city without a thought of remuneration and yet, when he was in need the city returned the favor. This lesson would stay with Ip Man throughout the rest of his life. He would seek to give what little he had. Often all he had to offer was his priceless Wing Chun, which he offered to those who showed honesty and sincerity of heart.

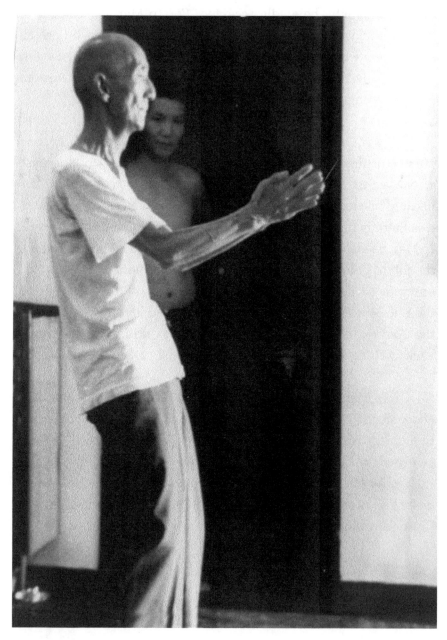

Ip Man engaged in the Siu Lim Tao form of Wing Chun while Ip Ching watches from the doorway.

Perfect Virtue

"When the love of superiority, boasting, resentments, and covetousness are repressed, this may be deemed perfect virtue." – Confucius

Grandmaster Ip Man always maintained that there are many people who boast about being the special student of a martial art genius, hermit or master of some sort. They brag about being the only person to have ever been personally taught the secrets or extraordinary skills of their particular art. Ip Man knew, all too well, that this type of detestable person likes using this sort of ploy to cheat his students and place himself on a larger than life pedestal. Ip Man also knew that those who engaged in such boasting had no confidence in what they actually learned, and were extremely shallow in the rules of martial arts. Moreover, a person of this caliber only wished to scare people by spinning this suspicious type of story. Such a person is doomed to fail from the very start.

Grandmaster Ip Man did more than express this sentiment; he lived it. Shortly after the end of the Japanese occupation, the city of Foshan found itself in dire need of a police force. Several men of ability and character were hired to serve as the police force in Foshan. Not the least of those hired was Grandmaster Ip Man. Because of his fame he was the logical choice in many people's minds for the position of Chief of Police. His skill coupled with the fact that the Communist Government was taking everything he owned, led Ip Man to accept the post as Police Chief. Thus began his first and only job as a hired employee.

Not long after the new police force began functioning, they were called upon to help solve a kidnapping. The police had a general description of the suspected kidnapper and his name but nothing more. Shortly after the beginning of the investigation, Ip Man, while walking through the park, spotted a man matching the general description of the suspect. The man was not more than a few strides ahead of Ip Man. Ip Man decided that he would call out the name of the suspect. If the man reacted, Ip Man would know that he had the right man and could bring him in.

Ip Man called out the suspect's name. The man turned and looked at him. Ip Man quickly closed the distance and attempted to apprehend the suspect. Pulling out a small revolver the man turned and thrust the gun at Ip Man. Ip Man quickly grabbed the cylinder of the revolver so that it could not rotate. Since his life depended on the cylinder not rotating, Ip Man exerted as much force as he could muster on the cylinder trapped in his grip. The pressure on the shoddy gun proved too much and the cylinder popped out of the revolver. Having fortuitously rendered the gun useless, Ip Man restrained and arrested the understandably startled suspect.

This account is worth pondering. Ip Man could have made this story into a much larger legend. He could have exaggerated the facts and embellished the story to raise it to a feat of legendary martial skill. He did nothing of the sort. There was no boasting and no embellishment. Although others have embellished this story, he always told the simple truth, letting the story speak for itself.

Lee Man and Grandmaster Ip Man. Lee Man was the first secretary at the Ving Tsun Athletic Association, and Grandmaster Ip Man was the lifetime Chairman.

Ip Man's honesty and transparency are the more insightful lessons of this story. Ip Man felt no need to embellish with the fantastic or mystical. So it was with the way he taught. Ip Man felt no need to hold to the mystical or quasi-mythical vocabulary that so often obscures the path of martial skill. He taught Wing Chun. It spoke for itself. The thing in itself, Wing Chun, was enough for Ip Man; he had no need for mystical fluff—no need for pedestal building. The truth is, confidence in himself and joy in the reality of Wing Chun kept him from wandering away in search of mystical greener pastures—pastures that were and are illusory.

Ip Man stands smiling in the center. His two sons Ip Ching on the far left and Ip Chun on the far right pose with him.

Grandmaster Ip Man, just after moving to Hong Kong.
Circa 1950

An Unwelcomed Necessity

Heaven, when it is about to place a great responsibility on a man, always first tests his resolution, wears out his sinews and bones with toil, exposes his body to starvation, subjects him to extreme poverty, frustrates his efforts so as to stimulate his mind, toughen his nature and makes good his deficiencies. Only then do we realize that anxiety and distress lead to life and that ease and comfort end in death.

—Mencius

Ip Man was a very powerful, wealthy, and famous man in Foshan. Yet during the years just before leaving Mainland China he became disenchanted with the puppet government that was soon to fall to Communism. Ip Man did not like the direction China was taking. He began looking for a better life. Just after the Japanese occupation of Hong Kong ended Ip Man permanently left Foshan and relocated in Hong Kong. He preceded nearly 750,000 other Chinese who fled mainland to Hong Kong in order to avoid the Communist take over.

No wealth to bring with him out of China, Ip Man lived in rooms or apartments he could afford to rent. It was during the early Hong Kong years that found Ip Man living in a very small room. Because he was accustomed to living and looking wealthy he did not want anyone to know where he was living. So anytime a person would ask where he lived, he just said, "I live at number 2 Boundary Street." But the fact was, this was an incomplete address. The address actually required a building letter in addition to a number, like 2A or 2B, and so on to the end of the alphabet. This meant that there could be twenty-six buildings with the number two in it, with hundreds of apartments in each building. Therefore no one could ever figure out where Ip Man lived. After many years, it became a standing joke. If you did not want anyone to know where you lived, you would just say you lived at number 2 Boundary Street.

For as long as he lived, Ip Man never again owned land, or a house. He left China in search of a better life. Even though he lost every worldly possession, there can be no argument, he found that better life after moving to Hong Kong.

An outside view of the apartment where Grandmaster Ip Man lived the later part of his life. This is the same place where I helped teach private classes for my father.

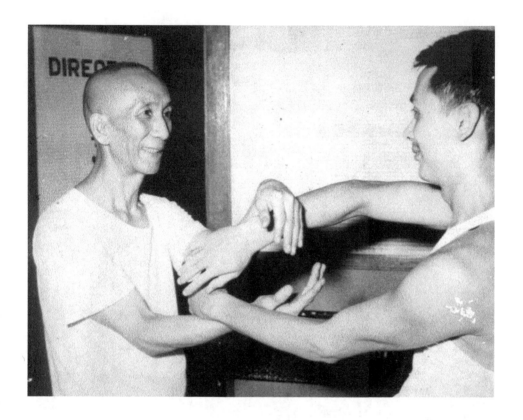

Grandmaster Ip Man and his student Wong Wing practicing Chi Sau. Ip Man always enjoyed Wing Chun and the workout it afforded him. He was able to practice the art right up until his death in 1972.

Honorable Character

*If wealth and honor do not dissipate you,
poverty and low status do not make you move from
your principles, authority and might do not distort
you, then you can be called a great man.*

—Unknown

Some say Ip Man sold Wing Chun, movement by movement. This is not true. Ip Man never did such a thing. He never exploited his students or his art. It is true that there are those who want to become rich in teaching and find that exploiting students is an easy way to accomplish this goal. Sometimes it becomes a mutual exploitation. The student thinks he can buy Wing Chun with money.

The ancient philosopher Mencius discussed this very point when he visited King Hui. The King thought that since this famous philosopher made a concerted effort to travel many miles to be granted an audience, then Mencius must surely want to discuss how to increase the profit of the kingdom. Mencius replied, "Why must you speak of profit? If you always say 'how can I profit my kingdom?' your top officers will ask, 'how can we profit our clans?' The common people will ask: 'how can we profit ourselves?' Superiors and inferiors will struggle against each other for profit, and the country will reduce in chaos."

By never taking advantage of his students, Ip Man preserved this ancient wisdom. When he passed away, he passed with nothing except the art that he loved so much. Grandmaster Ip Man's tuition in the early 1960s in Hong Kong money was 15.00 HK per month for his evening classes, and 10.00 HK for his afternoon classes. This was in a time when the average wage was around 200 to 250.00 Hong Kong per month. If one were lucky enough to be in the Bus Drivers' Union, or an employee of the Kowloon Motor Bus Company, Ip Man offered a discount.

Ip Man and some of his students.

Back in the 50's the Hong Kong government instituted the use of Identification Cards. These cards helped the residents of Hong Kong cross the border of Hong Kong and mainland China with no problems. Ip Man never truly owned any type of European or Western wear. He borrowed these clothes from a student and had the photo taken. The romanized spelling he used for these official credentials was Ip Man, the same official spelling used today.

What's In A Name?

To feed someone and not love them is the same as dealing with swine. To love someone but not respect them is like raising domesticated animals. Upon learning this, the superior man adjusts his conduct accordingly.

—Mencius

It is so difficult translating Chinese writing into romanization. There are two different schools of thought. The first school of thought is Pin-yin. The second one is Wade-Giles. Because there is still no actual standard way of writing romanized Chinese words, we have many misconceptions of spelling. For example, we just sound out the words Wing Chun. It could be spelled Ving Tsun because a ch sound in Chinese is a soft sound—not the hard ch like in the word child. And the V sound in English is actually a W sound in Chinese. If we went with the Wade-Giles spelling, then the Capital city of China would be spelled Pei-ching where the real pronunciation is something like Bay-jing. Since the sound is more important than the spelling, we have various spellings of the same word. Consequently everyone tries to phonetically spell Chinese words. This brings us to a very important issue—how to spell the Grandmaster's name. Most people are now spelling it Yip Man. This is totally incorrect. Even though they try to get across the proper sound, there is even a greater importance. This is the importance of protocol, the respect of elders, and of namesake. To change a proper name is to change the person himself. We cannot lose this protocol. Dealing with Chinese art, literature, culture, we cannot and should not assume too readily—no matter what the reason, no matter what the excuse. Adding a Y to the beginning of Grandmaster Ip Man's name is totally wrong. We must also remember that the Chinese say the family name first. This means that if Ip Man lived outside China his name would be Man Ip.

An early photo of Ip Man's student, Wong Sheun Leung, performing the first boxing set called Siu Lim Tao or Little Idea form.

Ip Man's student Chiu Van engaged in the pak sau movement from the second boxing form of Wing Chun.

Wong Sheun Leung (middle) and myself (far right). This is one of the last photos taken of Wong Sheun Leung before he passed away.

Ip Man had many influential friends. Standing next to the grandmaster in 1967 is the famous novel writer Hui Hoi Yu.

Grandmaster Ip Man, circa 1950

Finding The Soul

At first, my way with men was to hear their words, and give them credit for their conduct. Now my way is to hear their words, and look at their conduct.

— Confucius

The Great General Sun Tzu taught, "Know your enemy and know yourself; in a hundred battles, you will never be defeated. When you are ignorant of the enemy but know yourself, your chances of winning or losing are equal. If ignorant both of your enemy and of yourself, you are sure to be defeated in every battle." Ip Man understood this principle and used it in everyday life. He understood the inner person within each student. He was able to reach inside them and give them nicknames—not just any name but a name that fit each student, a name that revealed their very soul. For example, Ip Man lovingly gave the name The Three Braggers to three of his Hong Kong students—Yip Po Ching, Lok Yiu, and Wong Sheun Leung—who of course liked bragging in public about their kung fu prowess. Ip Man also gave the name Yat Ji Wong (meaning One Formula Wong) to Wong Sheun Leung. This name was given to Wong Sheun Leung because he would always give an herbal suggestion to his students or friends on how to cure an illness. His father was an herbalist and this helped Wong

Sheun Leung to figure out herbal remedies. However, Wong Sheun Leung always seemed to have only one formula. When the students came to Ip Man asking if Wong Sheun Leung knew what he was doing, the Grandmaster just said, "Well it can cure you, or it can kill you. You only need one formula." And so the name stuck.

This gift of nicknaming showed the Master-Disciple relationship that existed between Ip Man and his students. They were like a family. One could almost see a smile on the Master's face whenever he called his students by their nicknames—a smile that not only impresses in our minds that he understood the other person, but also that he understood himself. The master did not hide these names from his students. On the contrary, he delighted in using these special names. This shows great patience on his part for his students. In essence, Ip Man embraced his students, drawing them nearer in a relationship that formed an apprenticeship, or a powerful model of learning that celebrated the principle of "being," found in Wing Chun.

詠春之家成立同學第一次聯歡合攝民國四十二年十月

This early 1950's photo was taken in Hong Kong. It was the
grandmaster's students of the Restaurant Workers' Union.

Myself and my father, circa 1960

This photo is what the outside, front entrance to where my father and I lived during his later years, looks like. This is where I still live today.

Grandmaster Ip Man, photo taken at a photo studio in Hong Kong.

Three Dimensional Teaching

Learning without thought is labor lost; thought without learning is perilous.

—Unknown

Ip Man did whatever was necessary to teach a student. For example, he had a student with a very strong fear of fighting. So one day, to get his student over this fear, Ip Man took the student out on the streets of Hong Kong to look for a fight. While Ip Man and his student were walking down the street, Ip Man spotted a big Chinese guy—real tough looking. Ip Man thought this would be a perfect model of three-dimensional teaching. So, he started taunting the big guy into a fight by calling him mandarin face (because the guy had pitted skin like an orange peel). The big guy looked at Ip Man and his student, felt the courage in them, and got scared. After a few more seconds of Ip Man prodding, the big guy ran off. Did the master already know the big guy would run away? We are positive that the student did not know this bit of information. Did the master plan it this way? Maybe—maybe not. All we know is that if the big guy chose not to fight, then we learn that confidence wins out. On the other hand, if a person can be goaded into a fight (even by the Master), then we learn that this is wrong. Through this example, Ip Man provided his student, and us, with a three-dimensional model of learning that shapes our thinking about our fears, our growth and our relationship with the world.

Top left corner: Chu Shong Tin, Ip Chun, Wong Sheun Leung. Middle: Leung Sheung. Far right: myself and my father. Leung was my father's first student in Hong Kong and was one of the few people that my father told to open a Wing Chun school and begin to teach.

These two photos were taken at Ip Man's birthday party in 1967

A photo of one of the walls of the apartment where Ip Man lived. The above plate was a birthday gift to Ip Man from his student Moy Yat.

Another wall of the home of Ip Man displays a wonderful original painting of the grandmaster.

This photo is part of a set taken by Tang Sang in the school at Tai Yau Street in San Po Kong, circa 1967. Ip Ching recieved a copy of the negatives when Tang Sang asked him to arrange this set of photos. About two weeks before Ip Man passed away he made films of himself performing the forms with wooden dummy. He gave them to Ip Ching for safe keeping where they remain to this day.

These were the women of the Restaurant Workers' Union in Kowloon, Tai Nam Street. Ip Man did teach women the art of Wing Chun even though he joked about always having scratches on his arms from the workout.

Representatives of the Chinese Martial Art Association gather at the Ving Tsun Athletic Association for a friendly meeting, circa 1970. At one point during the Ving Tsun Athletic Association years the current administrator decided to change the agreement as to how much Ip Man was to recieve without talking it over with him first. This irritated Ip Man so much that he walked away from the Association with all of his students that could instruct classes, he stated that "It is not the money, it is the principle. You should have talked to me first." This left the Association in a terrible bind. So they enlisted the help of a rogue Wing Chun instructor. This caused an untrusting tension between this instructor and Ip Man for the rest of his days.

Teacher And Friend

Is it not delightful to have friends coming from distant quarters?

—Mencius

Sometimes if a master becomes too well aquainted with his students he loses his effectiveness as a teacher. And still other times, a master who is never a friend ostracizes himself from the student, making the student too afraid to come to the master with problems. Ip Man was a friend and a very effective master of Wing Chun. He loved socializing with his students. He would oftentimes go out late at night, and stay out until three or four in the morning—eating, laughing, drinking tea, or just visiting. He would then go home, sleep for about three or four hours, then wake up and go out for tea with some students. Then he would take a nap and wake up to teach his evening class until 10 p.m. and start the whole thing again.

In this, Ip Man found balance between the necessary respect for a teacher and the needed humanity of a friend. By finding this balance, Ip Man was able to enjoy life. This seems to be the case with all true masters. The Shoalin monks, after reaching a level of efficiency, left the temple to go out and teach the world. This is in direct contrast to most western ideas wherein the teachers, and even the holy men, holed up in temples and institutions, waiting for students to visit. They removed themselves from society so that they would appear to be like deity. Even Confucius rejected this hermit-like type of existence. So it was that as a friend and as a teacher, Ip Man exemplified the way of a master.

Left to Right: Yip Po Ching, Ho Luen, Grandmaster Ip Man, Chiu Van, myself, and my brother Ip Chun. Ip Man loved the outdoors and loved going out. Here we sit and enjoy each other's company at an outdoor restaurant at Tai Po Road, New Territory in Hong Kong.

Grandmaster Ip Man and his student Tang Sang, 1967

Grandmaster Ip Man circa 1970

Grandmaster, Ip Man

The Art of Noncompetition

To win one hundred victories in one hundred battles is not the acme of skill. To subdue the enemy without fighting is supreme excellence.

—Sun Tzu

As Sun-Tzu points out there is often an "other" orientation in martial combat. Martial artists often spend countless hours either trying to persuade others that they are better than other martial artists or they engage in competition to try and prove their superiority over the "other."

This "other" orientation, this pathological need to find our worth in comparison is beneath the true martial spirit. This pathological comparison, whether manifested as persuasion or competition, leads only to braggarts, cowards and marketing gurus; it never leads to martial mastery. Trying to convince a people of the superiority of something is detrimental to the true issues at hand. We live in an age where the power to communicate, influence and persuade, rule. There are those who can and do twist thoughts persuading others to believe one thing or that one person is better than another. We are subjects to the constant stream of character assassination that works people up to the point of obscuring vital issues, issues that could and would have changed lives for the better. Some assert competition is healthy, this is true, however they also assume that underhanded faultfinding, second-guessing, and evil speaking one of another is "healthy competition." The worst part of all this is, it influences people in epidemic proportions.

Grandmaster Ip Man said, "If you are a good teacher and martial artist, then students will find you. Those students that search you out will be dedicated and will make good martial artists. They are true and good people" For twenty years Ip Man taught in Hong Kong and never once advertised his school. He never put up a sign, or ran an ad of any kind. He felt that if an instructor advertised for students, he would have to accept everyone who came to him for instruction. Ip Man always maintained control of whomever, and whatever he did or did not teach. Without advertising, he could always be courteous in saying, "I am sorry but my class is filled. I cannot teach you at this time."

By not advertising Ip Man was able to get more dedicated students—students who were optimistic, outgoing, and would not adversely affect other students' learning. Ip Man always felt that it took a special student to overcome advertising ploys, and find Wing Chun, even though the odds were against it. It is not that Ip Man was against advertising; he was just against the pathological comparisons and improper motivations that came with it.

The non-competition philosophy also placed Ip Man in the unique position of never having to compete with any other martial art or martial art school. His competition was with himself alone, he always tried to be and do better than he was. Grandmaster Ip Man understood, with Sun-Tzu, that doing better than the next guy is at best only a temporary victory and at worst a delusion of the most dangerous sort. True mastery, true competition is a matter of the self.

Ip Man at my brother Ip Chun's wedding, circa 1965

*Enjoying the day with my father and kung fu brother
Yeung Wing*

Natural Understanding

"The twittering yellow bird rests on a corner of the mound." The Master said, "When it rests, it knows where to rest. Is it possible that a man should not be equal to this bird?"

—From the Chinese classic,
The Book Of Great Learning

There can be no argument that Hong Kong is a stark contrast of ancient and modern ideas, a collage that sets the senses reeling—color, sound, and nonstop movement. Although the Republic of China, the Sino-Japanese War, the Second World War, and the revolution of 1949 all rocked this tiny territory, they also provided new vigor, in the form of refugees who joined Hong Kong's teeming workplace. Known as the "City of Life" Hong Kong offers possibilities of mature learning that can only exist in hodge-podge cities of its kind.

It is the lot of a student to miss these lessons in favor of compartmentalizing and memorizing. However, it is a well-known fact that a master sees order in chaos, and principles everywhere he turns in life. Hong Kong itself became a schoolroom in Ip Man's eyes. As a witness to Hong Kong and China's past events, he was able to draw truth from any lesson life threw at him, no matter how simple it may seem. He filtered these things through his talent as a Wing Chun master, bringing to the surface greater talent and unseen dreams—which is the life of Wing Chun itself.

Ip Man loved walking through the streets of Hong Kong, he would walk alone or with students for hours on end. His ability to point to anything and give a Wing Chun lesson was amazing—anything from water to fire. In fact, Ip Man loved to watch fires. It was like a fight that needed to be controlled—a dangerous fight. Every time a fire broke out near where he lived in Hong Kong, his students who worked for the police department called him so that he could go and watch. Ip Man watched and learned—understanding how the principles of Wing Chun interact even with the elements and powers of life.

Grandmaster Ip Man with Yip Po Ching standing next to him, circa 1950. Yip Po Ching never had a school of his own, yet followed my father for over 15 years. He was a very dedicated Wing Chun practitioner. When Wong Sheun Leung first heard of Wing Chun he came to my father's school to challenge anyone he could find to a fight. It was Yip Po Ching who defeated him and convinced him that Wing Chun was the martial art he had been searching for.

Mr. Wong and my father at Mr. Wong's place of business, circa 1970. Mr. Wong was a very famous Fung Shui master and was my father's student.

*Grandmaster Ip Man with his student
Wong Wing (far right).*

Home at Tung Choi Street, circa 1968

The Right Measure

*The wise escape doubt; the good-hearted,
trouble; the bold, apprehension.*

—Unknown

Even though a student is taught how to kill in Wing Chun,
he is not taught to go out and kill. The student should be a smart
individual and should know how far to take a fight. Grandmaster
Ip Man knew very well how far he should go in a fight. After
training one night back in 1963, Ip Ching was feeling a little
hungry. So he asked his father if he wanted to go out for something
to eat. Ip Man thought it to be a good idea and accepted. They had
their late night snack and paid for it with a ten-dollar Hong Kong
paper bill. In those days a person could get a lot of food for one
Hong Kong dollar. But when the cashier gave Ip Man his change,
he gave it to him all in coins. Instead of putting the coins in his
pocket, Ip Man played with them in his hand. He continued to play
with the coins as he and Ip Ching left the building. On the way
home, four people surrounded Ip Man and his son. They acted
tough saying, "Old man, we have not eaten yet. How about letting
us have those coins?" Ip Man replied, "If you are going to rob us,
you need a knife, or brick, or something. How can you expect me
to give up this money by your talk alone?" Noticing the confidence
in both Ip Man and Ip Ching's eyes, the four men became fright-

ened and asked if they could just have the coins for a loan. Ip Man replied, "I do not know you. Why should I loan you any money?" The four men ran off.

Another incident happened after class one night when Ip Man, Ip Ching, Yip Po Ching, and a few other students went out for dinner. They went to a restaurant where Ip Man wanted to get a newspaper. Back in those days, there were no newspaper machines. The newspapers were just stacked on the floor. Ip Man bent down to get a paper in the crowd where a pickpocket was working. Ip Man had placed in his tunic breast pocket a very expensive fountain pen. This pen was the target of the pickpocket. He took it as Ip Man leaned over to get a paper. No one noticed but Ip Man, who did nothing just at that moment because of the awkward position. But as he leaned further down, he placed one hand on the stack of papers and kicked the man as he tried to make his escape. The kick made the man fly off his feet and land some 5 to 6 feet away from the group. Everyone was astonished. Ip Man calmly asked Yip Po Ching to go and retrieve his fountain pen for him. From this point on everyone knew the power Ip Man had in his kick.

For Ip Man the world was not a place to be feared. Ip Man's confidence was born of his knowledge of Wing Chun and his absolute faith in the ability of Wing Chun to protect him. Ip Man was a man of action. He saw what was right and he did it. In Wing Chun there is no hesitation, only right action.

Left to Right: My eldest sister Ip Ar Sum, my father, myself, and my wife Chan Miu Wah on my wedding day.

Ip Man at a restaurant.

1967, announcing the formation of the Ving Tsun Athletic Association. Left to Right: Grandmaster Ip Man, Lee Man, Leung Shong.

Left to Right: Chan Tau, Ip Chun, Grandmaster Ip Man. Chan Tau was the grandmaster of the Tao Style of Kung Fu. He was a good friend of my father's from Foshan. Mr Chan was the first person to suggest that my father open a school in Hong Kong.

The Steadfast Master

Nine things the superior person must be mindful of: to be clear in vision, quick in hearing, gentle in expression, respectful in demeanor, true in word, serious in duty, inquiring in doubt, firmly self-controlled in anger, just and fair when the way to success opens up.

—Unknown

We all stand at the stream of loyalty wanting the onrush to flood over us without our giving anything in return. But Ip Man knew all too well that loyalty does not flow in only one direction. It must, as love itself, flow openly between two people. Just like the spring is both the headwaters and the endpoint of the stream, loyalty gives rise to loyalty and love to love. If one desires loyalty, he must be loyal.

Ip Man demonstrated this principle over and over again with his unwavering loyalty to his sifu Chan Wa Shun. In fact, Ip Man never claimed anyone but Chan Wa Shun as his sifu. In return, Ip Man's students showed him loyalty and respect. With the exception of a few, Ip Man's students never claimed more than they knew and they never took advantage of their Sifu.

*Chow Lok Chi and Ip Man practicing chi sau
at our home, circa 1965.*

There was one student in particular who captured Ip Man's undying loyalty by never straying from his loyalty for him. Just before Ip Man died, he began to teach this student the most advanced part of Wing Chun, the Bot Cham Doe (to this day the most secretive part of the system). In fact, there were only five students Ip Man taught about the knives from beginning to end. This faithful student was very honored that Ip Man chose to teach him. It must be noted that practicing and teaching knives takes a lot of energy, and within a few days of classes, this student realized that Ip Man was being drained of energy after each workout. Desiring that his Sifu not be hurt in any way, the student made up an excuse that his business needed his attention and care. Upon hearing this Ip Man said, "You do not want to learn the knives? I will not be around much longer. What if I die before you can resume your studies?" He replied, "Sifu, since you began to teach me the knives and wished for me to learn them, if you do not live to finish teaching me the knives, I know that your son Ip Ching will finish teaching me."

This student demonstrated incredible loyalty. He gave up learning from the Master's hands to protect his Sifu. In the end, this student did not finish learning the knives from Ip Man. He finished his training through the grandmaster's son. But in the end, this student gained the spirit of Wing Chun's selfless service, complete loyalty and unfailing courage.

A recent photo, 1999, of the outside of the Ving Tsun Athletic Association in Hong Kong.

Grandmaster Ip Man

Ip Man's birthday party, 1967. Left to right, Grandmaster Ip Man, Chu Chung Man, Hui Hoi Yu.

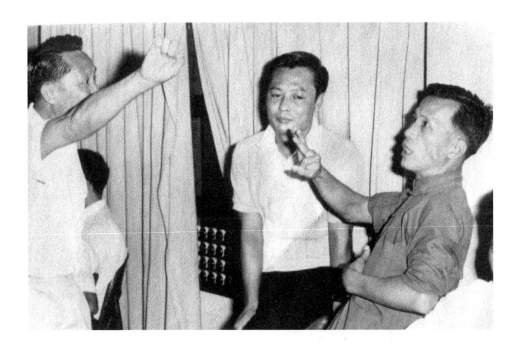

Some fun and games at the birthday party. Some of Ip Man's students enjoy each other's company. From left to right: Yip Po Ching, Wong Shuen Leung, and Chiu Van.

A great time with friends in the country. It was 1964 when we took this photo. Left to right: Chiu Van, Yip Po Ching, Ho Luen, Ip Ching, Ip Man and Ip Chun.

Ip Man's Gift To The World

Wherever the Superior Man passes through, people are transformed; the place where he tarried is spiritualized and Heaven and Earth blend harmoniously. How could you say 'he is gone'?
—Mencius

The gift that Ip Man left was a legacy of virtue and honor that is all too vacant in much of today's martial arts scene. Ip Man was born in China in 1893 and began his Wing Chun training around 1903. He was literally the link between the old ways and the new ways. He was the bridge that integrated the old ways of honor and virtue with a public martial art. Without Ip Man, Wing Chun would be lost today. Not only did Ip Man popularize Wing Chun to the point that the entire world wants to learn even the worst forms of it, but he was the only disciple to ever learn from Grandmaster Leung Jan's son, Leung Bik. Leung Jan only taught three people— his two sons (Leung Chun and Leung Bik) and Chan Wa Shun. Leung Chun never taught anyone. Leung Bik only taught Ip Man. Chan Wa Shun taught Ip Man and a handful of others. Ip Man learned the entire system intimately. Because of his Leung Bik lineage, he could have claimed the title of Grandmaster of Wing Chun. But he did not. Ip Man was tutored in martial virtue. Chan Wa Shun was his Sifu, even though he learned more from his later teacher, Leung Bik. In so doing, he honored his kung fu brothers, his teachers, and Wing Chun. Ip Man understood the role of tradition and honor in Wing Chun. It was his gift to the world.

Left to right wearing white sashes, Tang Sang and Leung Shong at Ip Man's funeral. Tang Sang was a student of Leung Shong's student but was able to get Grandmaster Ip Man to accept him as his personal student. This was the only time a student went from grand, grand student to a personal student. Tang Sang served as the president in the first year of the Ving Tsun Athletic Association, and was the head of Detectives in Hong Kong.

The funeral of Grandmaster Ip Man

The director of the Hong Kong Martial Art Association and a martial art delegation of all styles pay their respect to the grandmaster. As chairman of the Association Chan Hon Cheung leads the delegation.

The Hong Kong Martial Art Association delegation at Grandmaster Ip Man's funeral.

There were many people who loved and admired the grand-master. Here the movie star Shek Kin (of "Enter The Dragon" fame, in the dark suit) attends the funeral of Grandmaster Ip Man.

The burial ground ceremony

Grandmaster Ip Man's burial was held on December 8th, 1972. He was laid to rest in the cemetery at Fan Ling New Territories.

Ip Ching and a few of his students including Eric Li bottom left, pay their respects to Grandmaster Ip Man.

Ron Heimberger and Grandmaster Ip Ching at the gravesite of Grandmaster Ip Man.

This view is from the final resting place of grandmaster Ip Man, overlooking Hong Kong.

About the Authors

Ip Ching

Ip Ching's warm heart and humble personality has surprised many people in a world full of competition and ego. Ip Ching was born in 1936 in Foshan, China, the youngest son of the famous Wing Chun Grandmaster Ip Man. Most of the famous martial art masters lived in Foshan during the time Ip Ching was growing up. At the age of thirteen, Ip Ching began Wing Chun training under his father's guidance. However, his training was discontinued when his father moved to Hong Kong to try to find a better life for his family. Ip Man brought his eldest daughter with him to Hong Kong, leaving the rest of his children behind with their mother in China.

After Ip Ching graduated from high school, he attended college in Canton. In 1962, he moved to Hong Kong and was reunited with his father, once agian training and eventually finishing the Wing Chun system under his father's direct guidance.

Ip Man's school was at his house and Ip Ching lived with his father. This gave Ip Ching an enormous amount of insight into Wing Chun and his father's teaching methods. Because of this, he assisted his father, training students in the Wing Chun system until 1972 when Ip Man passed away. Ip Ching continues his father's traditions, teaching Wing Chun throughout the world.

A personal disciple of Grandmaster Ip Ching, Master Ron Heimberger is a world-renowned authority on the art of Wing Chun. He is President of the Wing Chun Kung Fu Council, with schools across North and South America, Europe, Middle East, and Asia. He is also a Director of the Ip Ching Wing Chun Athletic Association. Heimberger's ability and experience as a teacher are exceptional, a gift he attributes in no small part to his Master, Grandmaster Ip Ching; in addition to his vast experience teaching Wing Chun to martial artists, Heimberger has created specific programs of instruction for the military, law enforcement, and community organizations and is an accomplished instructional program developer. Heimberger is also an experienced author, having authored numerous works on diverse aspects of Wing Chun. As an author, martial artist and teacher, Heimberger is guided by his great passion and dedication to preserving and teaching the art and principles of Wing Chun.

Master Eric Li became a direct disciple of Grandmaster Ip Ching in September of 1973 while living in Hong Kong. In the early eighties. Li was elected as a director and worked as secretary of the Hong Kong Ving Tsun Athletic Association for three years. Then again he was elected to the same post in the early nineties. Li migrated to Vancouver, Canada in August of 1997. Li is a Director of the Ip Ching Wing Chun Athletic Association and spends most of his time teaching the art of Wing Chun.

INDEX
LISTING